Buyer Be~~ware~~...
Knowledgeable

The Self Empowerment of a Home Buyer

By Bud Miller

Note for Librarians: A cataloguing record for this book is available from Library and Archives
Canada at www.collectionscanada.ca/amicus/index-e.html
ISBN 1-4251-0752-4

PUBLISHING™
Offices in Canada, USA, Ireland and UK

Book sales for North America and international:
Trafford Publishing, 6E–2333 Government St.,
Victoria, BC V8T 4P4 CANADA
phone 250 383 6864 (toll-free 1 888 232 4444)
fax 250 383 6804; email to orders@trafford.com
Book sales in Europe:
Trafford Publishing (UK) Limited, 9 Park End Street, 2nd Floor
Oxford, UK OX1 1HH UNITED KINGDOM
phone +44 (0)1865 722 113 (local rate 0845 230 9601)
facsimile +44 (0)1865 722 868; info.uk@trafford.com
Order online at:
trafford.com/06-2510

10 9 8 7 6 5 4 3 2

DEDICATION

To my wife.

We survived this crisis
only because you are
so grounded and wise.
I thank God for you everyday!

You are
"The Wind Beneath My Wings!"

ACKNOWLEDGMENTS

Frank Dane, my friend and partner, thank you for wise counsel and encouraging me to dream my dream. Margi Dane and Susan Hall, we met at a time when Dee and I needed your fun hospitality and warm smiles: thank you for them. Cliff and Bobbie Greenlick, we cherish both of you. Dee and I love you and our friendship, which has grown year after year. Kenneth and Caroline Bailey, we have shared so many life cycle events together: Caroline, thank you for reminding me that when life hands you lemons "just turn it into lemonade." Kenneth, you are one-of-a-kind and a friend for life. Bob and Marty Bankhead, when the chips are down you are there: thank you. John and Myra Gevurtz, thank you for your friendship. The ocean air did help!

Our children are our treasures. They pulled us through this hard time! We love you Wendy, Bob, Elizabeth, Jamie and Scott.

Celeste Bennett, my editor, thank you for your ability to grasp the quirkiness of our experience and the passion and humor of my writing.

In memory, I offer love and respect to Emanuel and Bernice Miller, my parents, for my tenacity and sense of humor.

TABLE OF CONTENTS

FOREWORD

HOTEL HARD KNOCKS

Dear Family & Friends,

I trust that all is well with you. I wish I could say the same for me. Upon arriving at our new home, I found that we have been seriously misled by that charlatan of a contractor. While the site remains beautiful the home is <u>uninhabitable</u>, and it will take some months to repair.

The fact is, I have learned the hard way some essential information regarding home buying and building. After all is said and done...or not said and left unfinished...you are responsible for inspecting the condition of your future home. You may employ others to help you (as you know I did) but in the end it will be your signature on the Deed of Trust. Now there's a phrase that may be on the verge of extinction! Having been through the wringer, I tend to think signing a Deed of Trust is a little like sending a letter to Santa Claus. If it winds up in the right hands you'll probably get what you want; but if it winds up in the hands of an imitator, you will be sorely disappointed. You may just want to call it the Deed of Don't Trust.

I don't mean to frighten you away from buying or building, but I am writing this so you can save yourself the heartache and considerable expense of being misled. Be knowledgeable and be happy.

Love,

Bud

Dear Reader:

In this book you will find information, practical advice and an account of my "dream home" buying and building experience. I didn't know the ropes, and my dream home experience turned into a real nightmare. I am writing this book to catalog lessons I have learned, any one of which could save you a stay in the Hotel Hard Knocks.

Lesson one: buying or building a "dream home" requires that you stay wide awake! The romance and adventure of buying a home can be distracting. If nothing else, when making a visit (whether the first or hundredth visit) to your future home site, remember you are looking for what you don't want to see! Be sure to: 1) Stop, 2) Focus, 3) Adjust and 4) Educate. Always take a good friend, or somebody else not directly invested in the purchase.

In this book I suggest ways to establish boundaries that enforce productive, professional relationships with people who will influence your real estate transaction. For some of you, this will be asking you to be more persistent and demanding than your usual comfort zone allows. I urge you, in those moments, to recall the words of President John F. Kennedy, *"Let us never negotiate out of fear; but let us never fear to negotiate."*

Join me on this odyssey and do not assume it could never happen to you. Because that is what I said, and it happened to me. Read on and, please, learn from my experience.

And save lots of money, time and anxiety.

Sincerely,

Bud
Author & Homeowner

DISCLAIMER:

The author, being of sound mind, clearly states: I am not a know-it-all. And, in spite of having paid the price for a trip to hell and back (during which I met and identified many unseemly characters) I do not have the answers to any specific questions. I do not have the solutions for resolving any specific situations, nor do I have the ability to prevent the placing of obstacles in your path by charlatans serving their own self-interests. But I do have experiences from which you can draw wisdom, and I hope you will.

In keeping with tradition, names have been changed or withheld to protect the innocent. In a twist on tradition, names have also been changed to protect the guilty. For simplicity (and since the male liars, cheats, thieves, charlatans and incompetents we encountered during our odyssey seem to outnumber the females falling into one or more of those categories) we have followed the convention of using male pronouns throughout the text, unless the context specifically calls for the use of the female gender.

INTRODUCTION
THE STORY OF "BUD"

My name is Bud.

You should know that "Bud" is not my legal name. It's not an illegal name, but it is what I prefer folks to call me. Or maybe it's the name that I'm most often called. Or maybe I am getting too old to relate to the name my parents gave me and "Bud" is just easier. At any rate, the name "Bud" does not appear on any legal documents, nor has it been involved in any legal proceedings (many of which I speak about in this book). And therefore "Bud" is a safe distance from the name that was involved in a real estate misfortune during the first few years of this millennium. Although I intend to raise some eyebrows by telling the story of "Bud," I hope the unsavory characters that are depicted within the pages of this book will not recognize me. Because, you see, all of the characters in this book about real estate transactions are either based on real people or are an amalgamation of a small number of real people. And some of those people are just real mean; others are just incompetent.

Bud is not my real name, but I am a real person. I am just like you.

Well, maybe not exactly like you. But the point is that I am not unlike you. If you are reading this then it's likely that you are in the market for a new place of residence. Much like I was during the summer of 2001. This story describes some of the problems that I encountered that summer and some of the so-

1

lutions that I discovered in the following months. And some of the wisdom I've acquired over the course of my life.

I was raised in the greater Los Angeles area during the baby boom era of post-WWII America. I stayed in-state to attend college, and in 1970 I married a wonderful woman whom I met at UCLA. She has stuck with me for 35 years. Through all my dreamy and wide-eyed forays into entrepreneurship, she has stuck with me. She is practical, I am a dreamer, and we couldn't be more different. Either I am undeniably handsome and witty....or I am just really lucky. Either way, she is my partner and always has been. Together we purchased our first home, in Southern California, in 1972.

That was just before our first daughter was born, and within a couple of years we realized that we needed a bigger house. We sold our first home with a realtor, moved to Valencia, California and purchased our first brand new home in 1974. We both commuted from Valencia to Santa Monica: my wife for work and I for school. I can't tell you what the exact round trip distance was, but I think we all knew I must have been at least three-quarters out of my mind to choose a home that far from our daily destinations.

Two years later I became a licensed x-ray technician and like clockwork we got pregnant. This time it was twins. My new job was in Palm Springs, so we packed it all up and moved into a four bedroom rental house on a golf course in the California desert. We went to bed every night to the lullaby of coyotes howling from the nearby hills, a song that swept through the clear night air and swooped across the manicured fairways. And we awoke every morning to golfers shouting "fore" from the dog-leg of the fifth tee. Scorpions, red ants and rattlesnakes, oh my! My wife wanted out this time.

I found a job in Oregon, and we moved north. We rented a

house while exploring communities in which we might start our life as Oregonians. We contacted a realtor as a guide to this beautiful, rain-blessed state, where we hoped to land long enough to grow webbed feet.

About this time, I broke my foot playing racquetball. Wearing a knee-high cast, I worked nights at a local hospital and tried, during the day, to help raise our small army of children. Weekends were all about house hunting and asking our realtor hundreds of questions. We asked *so* many questions! We were still new to the home buying game, and we knew absolutely nothing about the area. Our realtor patiently found acceptable answers to every question we could dream up, and we eventually settled down in Lake Oswego, a town south of Portland.

Lake Oswego looked too good to be true, and you know what they say about that! I later learned that Lake Oswego was originally named Lake Sucker (true story) but was later re-named by developers trying to market the area as a high-rent district. It worked. Lake Oswego was beautiful. We went with our hearts instead of our brains. Or maybe we got a little impatient. Or maybe I got a little impatient, and my practical wife gave in to the dreamer in me. Not long after moving in, we wished we had asked our realtor a few more questions.

Our brand new house in Lake Oswego was constructed by a builder that, like us, knew nothing about the area and was on a tight budget. The home was built on soil that had a nasty habit of contracting and expanding as the seasons changed. The chimney outside the house cracked in half. We contacted the builder, who took a look then called to warn us to "keep out of the family room" until the bricks were removed and the chimney replaced. Our soil expansion research began when the new chimney cracked. After the fireplace cracked three times we ended up in court and had to summon the protection of our homeowner's policy. Remember the practical wife? Thankfully, she had purchased a homeowner's policy for $25.00. The repairs made to our home cost the insurance company almost 150% of our home's purchase price. We paid $61,000.00 to buy the home and the insurance company paid $87,000.00 to fix it. We lived in that Sucker Lake home for many years. That was the best $25.00 we ever spent.

Remember the 1980's, when it was a big deal to have a computer? The kids played games on "The Apple" at home. I was running my own business, and purchased a PC that I kept at the office. My wife spent long, lonely nights working on that PC. While out biking, we noticed a house which could accommodate our family and my office, plus provide some warehouse space. Yup, we moved.

Our new 5,500 sq. ft. house was perfect, but 10 years later the children were all college graduates with spouses, jobs and their own houses. It was time to shut down the business. It was time to downsize; time to move ourselves and 30 years of accumulated stuff.

By this time you would think I had learned enough lessons about home buying. No more leading with my heart! No more poor planning! After all the help we had received from realtors in the past, surely I would secure a realtor to help us in choosing the house in which we would retire! Sadly, I did not. We searched for...and found our new, smaller, empty-nester dream house. The rest of this book describes the expensive consequences of having entered into that transaction without professional objectivity.

The good news is that my mistakes are my mistakes. You, by reading this book, will be better equipped to avoid costly errors that I made. In the next few chapters you will see that what happened not only taught me about the real estate game, it also taught me about the nature of people who play in that game. Some players are on your side and some are not. The important thing is to know who is who and learn to recognize what everybody has at stake.

My name is Bud and I figured out how to win...the hard way.

CHAPTER 1
2 OF 10: THE BANKERS

New home in your near future? If you are like most people, you will need a loan. So...probably even before you begin to look at properties...off to the bank you will go. If you are like most people you will not find this a case of "laughing all the way to the bank." In fact, you may find yourself fixing your hair, checking it three times in the rear-view mirror, clearing your throat and rehearsing your loan request in several different tones of voice. You may even feel an urge to cry. At the very least, you can expect butterflies in the stomach and a not-so-steady feeling in the knees. Asking for money is never easy, and this is a lot of money.

Once at the bank, you will visit the Loan Officer...or "Loan Consultant," or "Loan Advisor" or "Counselor." There are numerous titles for this person, who will be sitting at a desk off to the side of the tellers. Applying for a loan is anything but an everyday event for you, but for the loan officer it is business as usual...possibly even the low-light of a boring afternoon. So my advice to you is: relax. Mind you, I'm hardly capable of heeding my own advice, but for what it is worth, you will be better able to listen if you settle down and take a professional stance.

In my case, the loan officer sat behind an enormous mahogany desk with a little placard that bore her name. That placard should have read, "**1 of 10**."

For every loan officer you meet there will be at least nine other people in other branches and offices (in other states) who will evaluate and process your application. Think of the person behind the mahogany desk as their Talking Head. **1 of 10** will be, effectively, the front person for many faceless, impersonal cogs working in a financial conglomerate that will be handling or mishandling many responsibilities associated with the purchase of your new home.

The loan officer will chat with you a little and ask you, as a matter of obligation, about your life. It will all seem very polite and fake, but you should be expecting that. **1 of 10** will furnish you with a loan application packet, some numbers, more chit chat, more numbers including the current interest rate, even more chit chat, advice on filling out the application and a well-rehearsed personal story about his uncle and a boat and some kind of loan. Or maybe you'll get a story about a sick dog or a child's birthday party...at any rate, you will get 30-45 minutes of this person's time, some forced courtesy and absolutely no useful information. Within ten minutes of leaving the bank, every figure and fact quoted to you may have changed. Except for the dog that ate the Christmas lights and threw up on the lawn...some things never change.

It is likely that you will make more than one trip to the bank. The first application is usually to pre-qualify: the bank reviews your application and determines how much it is likely to lend you. Its answer is what allows you to begin looking at properties that you know will be in your budget.

Unless you omit a digit of your Social Security number or misspell your mother's maiden name, it is unlikely that you will hear from **1 of 10** again until your loan application has been accepted or refused.

If your first application is accepted, your second appointment at the bank most likely will be to complete a packet of forms that will be the basis of your actual loan; a loan secured by the property you want to purchase. Since you went through the pre-qualification process relatively recently, this new packet will look familiar. It is actually an entirely new packet of applicatory forms and related gobbledygook. You will have to sign and date all these forms. You may have to hear the dog story again.

This time it gets a little more complicated. Your appointment with **1 of 10** may be at 10:00 AM, but it cannot be completed until **2 of 10** returns from lunch. **2 of 10** works in an office two time zones away and has been enjoying a well-deserved break and a bento bowl in his midsize sedan.

Upon returning from lunch, **2 of 10** will call your insurance company to confirm that you have taken out homeowner's insurance and that the bank is protected from any harm that may come to the property securing your loan.

Naturally, you have already secured homeowner's insurance! Because you are a responsible adult and that is what responsible adults do: we insure things. Your insurance agent confirms to **2 of 10** that your new insurance will start on a specific date and time…let's say, July 3, 2001 at 12:01 AM.

Now, until the first week of July, 2001, I always considered insurance to be a method of securing "peace of mind" while complying with the laws of the land. I was a glass-half-full kind of guy. So when my insurance agent assured me that my new house was insured I had my "peace of mind," and I went on my merry way. I was not worried about protecting myself. I had complied with the rules, I had chosen a reputable company, and I trusted my agent. My house was insured. Right?

Wrong.

What I should have done was: gotten my insurance agent's signature stating the date and time the policy became effective. I should have had the insurance policy notarized. I should have requested...no, <u>demanded</u> a return FAX from the insurance company stating that my funds had cleared, that my business had been accepted, and that my policy was active and in order. I should have known better than to trust the spoken word of a business associate, albeit one with whom I'd done business for fifteen years. I should have protected myself.

What I should have done: I didn't do.

Remember **2 of 10**? Well, **2 of 10** had a hot date, or some other pressing engagement the night of July 2, 2001. Maybe he was planning on getting an early start on washing the bento stain out of a favorite shirt. I can't be sure. But, on the afternoon of July 2, 2001, **2 of 10** had arranged to leave work early. He assumed the loan would not close before the holiday. Realizing that July 4th was near and that a house cannot close on a national holiday, **2 of 10** did the responsible adult thing. **He** called my insurance agent and un-insured my new house.

I am certain that **2 of 10** must have thought, "Why should the homeowners have to pay for insurance on a house that they do not yet own?" Each day of insurance would have cost us $18.00. Without consulting us, **2 of 10** instructed my insurance agent to bind my insurance policy over to start at 12:01 AM on July 5, 2001. That decision saved us $36.00 and almost cost us hundreds of thousands...but more about that later.

2 of 10's job was done for the day. So on July 2, 2001, after un-insuring my new house, **2 of 10** passed my file to **3 of 10**.

3 of 10 was also in a hurry to tie up all loose ends and get out of the office to enjoy a well-deserved holiday. So **3 of 10**

made sure that **2 of 10** and **1 of 10** had checked all the correct boxes and that all the necessary signatures, initials and dates were in place. And on the way out the door, **3 of 10** plunked my file on **4 of 10**'s desk.

4 of 10 called the escrow company to confirm that all of its boxes were checked and that it had all of the compulsory signatures, certificates, initials and dates. With everything in place, **4 of 10** passed my file on to **5 of 10**.

5 of 10, having just received the Certificate of Occupancy, was satisfied with my file, so he called **6 of 10** and requested that the funds be transferred.

7 of 10 wired the money to **8 of 10** by 5:00 PM on July 2, 2001.

9 of 10 recorded the title by e-mail to **10 of 10** and at 4:41 PM on July 3, 2001, the home was OURS.

That evening, our realtor called us and invited us to come and get the keys to our brand new house. CONGRATULATIONS! At 5:10 PM on July 3, 2001 we became the proud owners of a house that was to be uninsured until 12:01 AM on July 5, 2001.

About 8:00 PM on July 3, 2001, faulty plumbing, poorly installed by an unscrupulous builder, caused 5,840 gallons of water to flood the house over the course of two hours.

Our brand new house was nearly destroyed. And we soon found out that our house was not insured! All because **2 of 10** acted on our behalf, and because we had not known enough to protect ourselves from the fallout of decisions made by faceless, impersonal cogs.

NOTES:
2 OF 10: THE BANKERS

CHAPTER 2
KNOW THE CODE: CHOOSING A REALTOR

Buying or selling a home can be tricky. And I don't just mean that it is complicated. In fact, *"complicated"* may be an understatement. Attempting to sell your home, with the intention of getting a decent return on your real estate investment, while trying to organize the relocation of your family can be a three ring circus! Considering that your house may be one of your most expensive investments, both fiscally and emotionally, it is wise to hire a professional to run the show. And realtors are some of the hardest working people in show business.

Your realtor will play many roles: he will deliver an effective sales pitch, manage the set-dressing of an open house and pace the dramatic finale as he hands you the keys to your new home. Your realtor is not only the driving force behind the scenes: he also plays the lead role, and probably with a good deal of style.

Now, before you get the impression that I have an unusually high opinion of the average realtor, let me ask one question: why employ an average realtor? Never settle for *run-of-the-mill*...when you can get *outstanding*. I recommend that you interview several realtors and hire the best.

➔ Ask all the people you know whether they have had a successful relationship with a realtor. Many people have relatives in the business, but your secretary's cousin is not necessarily the best choice. I have a cousin who I wouldn't trust to sell an umbrella. Ask your acquaintances *why* they would recommend their realtor.

→Do your homework. Check the local newspapers for realtors who are dedicated to your region or neighborhood-of-interest. Check with your State's Association of Realtors.

→Choose a full-time realtor. You shouldn't trust your house to a part-timer, moonlighter or hobbyist. Your house is probably your biggest investment, and it deserves the attention of a full-time professional.

→Choose and set up appointments with three or four realtors who seem to be the best match. Try to select realtors from different companies: this may spark some competition for your business.

→Set the tone by being confident and sincere. Ask a lot of questions. Write down the realtor's answers. Remember that you are conducting an interview. Ask for references. Be sincere and straight-forward. You are doing the hiring.

→If you are selling, you may want to let each interviewee know you will make a decision only after you've assessed all offers. You are doing the hiring.

→Choose a realtor who is successful, knowledgeable, likeable and honest.

Realtors can be defined by what they do. They help people like you and me buy and sell houses. But they can also be characterized by HOW they do it. Realtors have a Code of Ethics. Not an unspoken, common knowledge, old-wives-tale type of ethical code. Realtors have an official "*Code of Ethics and Standards of Practice*" under which they practice their profession. Your realtor should know this code. It is not enough to trust a mere shuffler of real estate to handle affairs related to the buying or selling of a home. Hire a person who can excel at the task and do so with integrity[1].

---

[1] See page 82.

From the *Realtor Code of Ethics and Standards of Practice, 2005:*

> *The term REALTOR® has come to connote compe-*
> *tency, fairness, and high integrity resulting from ad-*
> *herence to a lofty ideal of moral conduct in business*
> *relations. No inducement of profit and no instruction*
> *from clients ever can justify departure from this ideal.*
>
> *In the interpretation of this obligation, REALTORS®*
> *can take no safer guide than that which has been*
> *handed down through the centuries, embodied in the*
> *Golden Rule, "Whatsoever ye would that others*
> *should do to you, do ye even so to them."*
>
> *Accepting this standard as their own, REALTORS®*
> *pledge to observe its spirit in all of their activities and*
> *to conduct their business in accordance with the tenets*
> *set forth below...*

The *Realtor Code of Ethics*, in its entirety, goes on for pages and pages.

I don't think that I realized the level of personal investment realtors make until I started researching this book. In Appendix B you'll find a website address for the complete *Realtor Code of Ethics*. Before selecting a realtor, you may want to read the code to increase your awareness of the guidelines under which a professional realtor operates.

To be successful, realtors must have a high level of personal commitment. The *Realtor Code of Ethics* illustrates the standards to which realtors are held.

NOTES:
KNOW THE CODE: CHOOSING A REALTOR

CHAPTER 3
MY NAME IS THURSDAY:
CHOOSING A CONTRACTOR

The following is a story...an almost true story. As is acceptable in historical fiction, many of the details have been exaggerated and some of the details are just plain made-up. The names have been changed to shield the guilty, scum-sucking crooks that are portrayed. Any similarity between the despicable villain in this story and the builder we contracted to construct our dream house is not coincidental and is, in fact, intended solely for the amusement of everyone.

This is the city...the city that rarely sleeps-in past 6:30 AM. It's not a hard city or a wicked city; it's a city where, if you find a newspaper on a park bench, the crossword puzzle has probably already been removed. It's a crafty city. You've got to stay on your eyes and keep your toes peeled. This is the city where I do my job.

It was a standard day in the city. Things were neutral at best... until I received a telephone call from a distraught homeowner. When I say "distraught," I mean irritated to the point of nostril flaring.

I said, "Thursday here."

I always answer the phone expecting to receive a take-out order for kung pao chicken, because my phone number is one digit away from Jin's House of Joyful. But all I heard was nervous breathing. This time there would be no request for extra dipping sauce: this was an actual victim on the line.

"I don't know if it's going to be the builder, the banker, the escrow agent or the realtor," he said, passionately. I could hear the sound of nostrils flaring.

"Candlestick maker?" I offered. He paused for a moment and this time, I could hear his eyes roll.

"...but somebody is responsible for the flood, and..."

Okay, I know what you're thinking. Floods are an act of God, right? That was the notion I had. So I interrupted again as I broke into loud laughter...which was just exactly the degree of annoying needed to trigger the victim's "outrage" mechanism. He began screaming.

"GOD MAKES RIVERS FLOOD...NOT #% *@$ HOUSES!"

As it turns out, his brand new dream dwelling had been damaged by flooding; from the inside-out. He had received the keys at 5:10 PM and by 8:00 PM his dreams were under water. 5,840 gallons of city water had virtually destroyed his house. So I stopped laughing. Because this is my job.

My name is Thursday, and I'm a cop. Okay, *technically*, I'm waiting for my private investigator's license application to be approved. But, until then, I am assisting victimized homeowners... *vigilante style*.

I went with the homeowner to visit his personal state of catastrophe and survey the impairment of his hacienda. It was wet.

Relying on experience, both real and imagined, I figured that the first thing to do is calm the victim. Since I had already missed the boat on that opportunity I went directly to Phase Two: I asked the victim what had happened. It turns out that the victim didn't know what had happened. That is why he hired me.

From the homeowner's gestures I construed the whereabouts of the swamp/house builder. The builder, a Mr. Liarson, lived near the victim. I paid the home of Mr. Liarson a visit.

I found Mr. Liarson sitting on the front porch showing all the liveliness of an indolent door stop. I'm not suggesting that the sluggish creature was completely brainless, but his facial expression was startlingly blank. It conveyed a sense of futility, and gave me mild indigestion. I asked the man if he had any information concerning the flood. He either knew nothing or was too occupied with sucking lunch remains out of his teeth to bother responding.

Suddenly, I heard vicious metallic grinding noises issuing forth from Mr. Liarson's home. I brushed past the imbecile on the front porch, burst into the Liarson estate and dramatically whipped off my sunglasses. There, through an open door that led to the home-office of the Liarson residence, I saw a woman in a rage of torment, panic and guilt. She was at the desk, crying and feed-

ing parts of an electric type-
writer through a paper shredder.
This had to be Mrs. Liarson, and I
immediately suspected that she was
the brains of the operation.

Okay, like I said, that was an *almost* true story. Our new dream house did get flooded with 5,840 gallons of water, our builder did live close by, and he has indeed been the cause of indigestion.

The builder's wife was also probably the "brains of the operation," but more about her (and how to identify an authorized representative) later.

Choosing the right builder to build your new home is obviously an important decision. In every group of honest professionals there is a "Mr. Liarson." This is true about every profession but is especially dangerous when a professional's work involves asking clients to invest a good chunk of their life savings. Do not do business with the "Mr. Liarsons" of the world.

Mr. Liarson operated in a self described "learn as you go mode." What he lacked in professional home-building training and experience he more than made up for with his desire to profit. The end product was a poorly built home, an accident of mammoth proportion and a messy cover-up.

It is a bad sign when the builder and his wife attempt to mop up 5,840 gallons of water in the hope that you may not notice some of the water marks on walls a floor below. That Mr. & Mrs. Liarson did so was reported to us by an honest workman who was installing equipment two floors below the burst pipe when the floodgates opened. Mr. & Mrs. Liarson's attempts to mop up and hide evidence of the flood indicates, in hind sight, a level of panic that points to their financial instability. If we'd just checked their credit reports before selecting a house which they had built....

CHOOSING A CONTRACTOR

Your building contractor will be the one to define the process. Nevertheless, you will be putting on a "do-it-yourself" homebuilder hat when you choose a contractor. Inexperienced and/or under qualified contractors can cost you a lot of money and chip away at your sanity. I've developed a system to help you prevent these losses by finding reputable contractors.

The **first step** is to prepare a list of candidates. I highly recommend ignoring the fact that your next-door neighbor claims to be a contractor. Begin by asking friends, relatives and coworkers to tell you about contractors who have done good work for them. Do some investigating: discover where local contractors buy their raw materials and ask those wholesalers for recommendations. If you're buying new property ask your realtor: realtors often know which builders do the best work in the area.

The **second step** is to narrow the list by determining which contractors are people with whom you want to do business. Interview all of the contractors on the list. Write down your questions beforehand. Take notes, or invite someone else whose sole task will be to take notes during the interview.

INTERVIEWING CONTRACTORS

➜ Ask how long he has been in business as a contractor. In other words, "How many houses have you built?" You don't want to be the first job.

➜ Ask what responsibility the contractor assumes for work done by subcontractors. Who will fix any problems: the contractor, the subs, or an insurance company's contractor? Most contractors hire people to do specialized work: plumbers, electricians, etc. It is imperative that you find out who will be ultimately responsible for the finished product!

→ Ask what amount of liability insurance the contractor has available.

→ Ask the contractor whether he has any complaints filed against him with the Better Business Bureau (BBB) and then call the BBB and confirm the answer.

→ Find out whether the contractor belongs to the local builders association and whether or not he belongs to the National Association of Home Builders.

→ Ask about his policies on post-construction walk-throughs. Tell the contractor you want to live in the house before the final walk-through. (See pp. 33-34.)

→ Require that potential contractors provide a list of clients, and then take time to interview these people. Ask, "Did the contractor finish the project on budget and on time?" Most importantly, ask "What went wrong? How did he respond?"

After the interview, review the written notes and ask yourself: "Did the contractor communicate well? Do you like him?" If you don't like him personally, do not expect to like working with him professionally.

Once you narrow down your list to contractors that meet your qualifications, you can move on to the **third step:** asking each one to submit an official bid on how much the project will cost. To do this, write a letter informing each qualifying contractor that he is on your list of finalists. (It is okay to tell the contractors how many bids you will be considering.) You may want to summarize the interview questions and answers, asking each contractor to confirm you have a correct understanding of the answers he gave. For best results, get bids from at least three contractors. Be prepared for bid preparation to take some time. If done properly, a bid can take weeks to complete.

The **fourth step** is comparing the contractors' bids:

→ Base your decisions on the specifications and detailed plan.

→ The bid should be clear and well organized. A proper bid will not just be a number written on a scrap of paper.

→ Meet again with the contractors. Ask as many questions as you need to gain an understanding of what the contractors intend to give you for your money.

→ Before this second meeting, write down your questions. During the meeting, write down the contractor's answers. After the meeting, write a letter summarizing both and asking each contractor to confirm you have a correct understanding of his answers.

When reviewing the bids remember that many things go into a house: many objects, devices, surfaces, treatments and materials. And, it turns out, there are as many options as there are different things. Review the options with your builder to make sure he includes options you desire. Working closely with your builder and asking a lot of questions can help him to make choices that will best suit your preferences. You, not your builder, will be living in the finished product, and the builder should be willing to put anything you want into your house.

The **fifth step** is to choose your contractor, and then you both must sign a contract. That contract is to protect both parties, even though the contractor or his legal representative will probably draw up the contract. Read the contract carefully, and make certain that you understand it. Read the contract looking for the following necessary items:

- →Date the work will be started. Date the work will be completed.

- →Signed copies of all permits and inspection reports will be provided.

- →Stipulation that a written warranty of workmanship will be provided.

- →Any and all promises made by the contractor.

- →What quality, grade and brand of materials will be used.

- →What quality, grade and brand of appliances will be used.

- →What penalties will be paid to you if the work is not completed on time.

- →Who will clean up and/or remove debris from the job site.

- →What provisions will be made for you to make changes and how the cost of changes made will be determined.

- →The total amount you will pay the contractor.

- →A schedule of how and when payments will be made.

- →Your right to terminate the contract.

Before signing the contract, visit a home the selected contractor has completed.

Even if all items are present, there is one crucial point to remember: **authority** is a big word. Authority allows people to do big things. Promises and decisions made by someone without authority are, legally speaking, just meaningless breezes or the proverbial "sweet nothings." In dealing with our builder, we learned that even the most reasonable-sounding promises can be promptly broken, without legal recourse, if made by someone who does not have proper legal authority.

Case and point: *The Builder's Wife*. Recall, if you will, Thursday's description of the lovely creature that was last seen force-feeding office machinery into an overworked paper shredder. That would be the woman who our builder, Mr. Liarson, chose as his partner in crime...er, I mean...*business partner*. Mrs. Liarson, after taking off the bridal veil, began wearing many hats. In addition to clean-up and document disposal services, she provided "business management." We also think she worked part time as a surveillance officer, explosives expert and cat burglar...but we can't prove that. As the business manager, she was ready, able and willing to make most of the decisions and promises for her and her husband's home wrecking... er, I mean...*home building* business. Not all of her decisions and promises held up.

During the finishing phase of our dream home's construction, our realtor contacted us to deliver some news: the flooring for most of the house was installed and ready to go, but the bonus-room was still floorless. This room was to be my wife's sewing room. She is a sewing enthusiast and knows that pins and rugs and feet don't get along well. We wanted to make the bonus-room flooring choice. We promptly hit the road to visit the mega-flooring-warehouse. We were glad to have the opportunity to pick something we really loved!

We chose a floor. We called the builder. Mrs. Liarson answered our phone call. The builder was unavailable. The flooring company representative was familiar with Mr. & Mrs. Liarson and had actually worked with the Mrs. several times in the past. The details of our new bonus-room flooring were communicated, and Mrs. Liarson approved the purchase and installation.

Remember…authority is a big word.

While signing a million pieces of legal documentation at the escrow office a few weeks later, we were informed that there had been a price misunderstanding. *A price misunderstanding?* We found that the builder's wife had misunderstood the square footage and had misquoted the available allowance to the floor salesman. We were then told that we would have to come up with the difference, out of our own pockets, if we wanted the house.

But the builder's wife approved it!

Yes, she approved it, but she had *no authority* **to do so.** A track record with the mega-flooring-store's order clerk does not an authority make. In actuality, the builder's business manager was not legally authorized to be involved with any of Mr. Liarson's business dealings. Legally-speaking, Mrs. Liarson was just his spouse.

Make sure that promises and decisions made about your personalized choices are made with the proper authority behind them. **These are questions that must be asked and answered**:

➔ Does your builder's representative have the authority to make changes to the materials being used by one of his subcontractors?

➔ Will the changes being made add or subtract from your cost?

Consult an attorney if you would like help comprehending the contract and its terms. Be aware of your obligations. In every state, there is a period in which you may change your mind. In some states you have three days in which you may legally rescind the contract without penalty.

If you follow these guidelines and take the task of choosing a contractor seriously you will likely get satisfactory results.

BUD'S FIVE RULES
OF CONTRACTOR MAINTENANCE

1. Determine who has the authority to make changes and only deal with that person when requesting a change from the original plan.

2. Study the materials, surfaces, treatments, structures and appliances that will go into your new house.

3. Make a personal list of the top five things you want added or changed, and focus strongly on those items when meeting with contractors to review bids.

4. Always document an authorized change. Be sure these change orders are signed and dated by an authorized contractor representative. Be sure the form identifies in what capacity the company has vested the signatory with change-making authority.

5. Always request the 3/4 horsepower (or better) garbage disposal and a professionally-installed garage door opener. The typical spec disposal will have trouble grinding celery, and having "after market" garage door changes made is expensive and not covered by your home warranty. Even if you pay for an upgrade, have your builder install it. Installations made afterwards, by other vendors, will not be covered by your home warranty.

NOTES:
MY NAME IS THURSDAY:
CHOOSING A CONTRACTOR

CHAPTER 4
7 DEADLY SINS: ASSESSING CHARACTER

1) Trust me.

2) You have my word.

3) I give you my solemn promise.

4) Consider it done.

5) Believe me!

6) You know I'm an honest person.

7) Do you want to hear the truth?

When it comes to real estate the last thing you want to hear is the sound of a professional trying earnestly to convince you of his honesty. Trust is not something that is bought or sold; it is earned. No amount of haggling will increase a person's ethical standards. In fact, I suggest to you that a person who finds it necessary to sell himself as reputable probably isn't.

This chapter lays out clues for knowing when to walk away. For most of us, real estate represents the largest investment we have the ability to make. Transactions involving your life's savings should be conducted with people of good character.

This is not a time to be concerned with forging life long friendships. This is not the time to display your ability to trust. Real estate transactions must be dealt with using the protection of standard business practices.

When dealing in real estate it is imperative that everything...and I mean EVERYTHING...that is discussed becomes part of a written document. Or more specifically, a **signed, dated, time-stamped** and **witnessed written document**. Assume nothing.

If demanding documentation makes you appear to be an untrusting cynic, then so be it. You'll just have to get over the stigma of shrewdness. There are a lot of sharks out there, and shrewdness is a good way to protect yourself and your family from those that make a living ingesting other people's assets.

The following suggestions offer some protection from deceptions:

➔ Get it in writing. If it is not in writing, the conversation never happened.

➔ Tie down dates. The statement, "consider it done," is a bold faced lie.

➔ Never accept "no problem" as an answer...get a "yes" or "no."

➔ Never agree to provide NON-REFUNDABLE money without a clause holding the seller equally accountable.

Let's talk about pledging non-refundable money. Never allow yourself to be bullied into committing your hard-earned cash on a fool's gamble. If the other party requires you to deposit money that he is allowed to keep no matter what happens, you need to negotiate a clause that requires him to pay a penalty if the seller or other parties breach the contract.

If your realtor tells you that you must put down earnest money to secure your chances of buying a home, insist that your deposit be 100% refundable. If the seller will not accept those terms, offer to increase the amount of earnest money that you are willing to deposit but insist on retaining the right to a complete refund. If the seller still will not accept your terms, consider carefully whether you really want to do business on his terms. If you decide to proceed, tell your realtor you want to add a contract clause that will penalize the seller by an off-setting amount, or percentage of deposit, if he breaches the contract.

Please consider these recommendations regarding earnest money:

➔ Be prepared to put down a healthy deposit.

➔ A deposit of $5,000.00 followed by an additional $10,000.00 within 48 hours is usually enough to communicate that you are serious. If the seller is asking you to put down non-refundable money, you need a penalty clause that holds him accountable for any breach of the contract. Until you are financially secure enough and/or confident enough to be prepared to offer this kind of deposit, you might not be seen as truly serious about the property involved.

➔ Under no circumstance will you allow any of your deposit money to be moved to a non-refundable status without an equally offsetting clause holding the seller accountable. You must keep leverage on your side as you progress through negotiations, inspections and contingencies.

➔ No matter how persuasive his reasoning, if a seller is asking you to move any part of your deposit to a non-refundable status, be sure your interest in the deposit is protected by an equally strong clause that will penalize the seller for breaching the contract.

➜ All of your deposit money must stay in a safe escrow account. That is an escrow account not controlled by the seller. No exceptions.

➜ If a selling party keeps trying to talk you into non-refundable money, be aware that you might be dealing with a shark or a desperate person.

It is tempting to get caught up in the romance, excitement and adventure of buying a new house. But you must keep your eyes, ears and options open to the facts.

If you are depositing money on a house that is being built for you, apply the above recommendations and make some additional demands:

➜ At escrow, set up a substantial "hold back" account. The standard hold back is one-fourth of the contract price. You will hold back $25.00 for every $100.00 of the contract price. You must do this or you will have ZERO leverage when it comes time to take possession of your newly constructed house.

➜ When establishing contract terms demand three walk-throughs with the builder.

➜ Before the first walk through, visit the home during various hours and weather conditions. Look at your new house in bright sunshine, at dusk, while it's raining and even at night. Visit your new house when it's cold and when it's hot. You will be surprised how varying circumstances change what you see in your new house.

→ Before the first walk through hire a private home inspector to help you develop a punch list. The money you will spend to hire a private home inspector is a necessary expense. You cannot trust the builder to be forthright about the condition of the work he has done or contracted out. You must hire your own inspector. Find an objective inspector: do not hire an inspector that works with your builder or is associated with a realtor involved in the deal. Ask the inspector what items will not be inspected. Make sure that the home inspector's report becomes part of the initial punch list.

→ Take the next walk through with the builder, as a prerequisite to taking possession of the house.

→ Negotiate a clause that includes a final walk-through twenty days after taking title and establishes an escrow account to retain a percentage of the price of the house to cover unfinished or unsatisfactory work. Then live in the house for twenty days and take notes. (See Choosing a Contractor, pp. 22-23.)

→ The **punch list** will describe every correction that the builder must make before you will state that the house was built to the agreed upon specifications. The punch list must be agreed upon, signed, dated and time-stamped by the builder. The builder will not receive "hold back" money until the punch list items have been resolved.

→ If a builder will not agree to working within these rules...do not do business with him. Walk away. A reputable builder will want to be proud of his completed project's workmanship. You cannot deal with a builder who will not accept the fact that most houses need minor adjustments after completion. Find another builder who has faith in his ability to deliver according to plan.

Remember: in assessing someone's character be professional. Professional means setting standards and acting to achieve them. Politely demand that your interests be protected. If being nice conflicts with being professional, choose "professional."

Check, double check and triple check everything. Trust no one to deliver without documentation. Ninety-nine percent of the paperwork you sign when completing a real estate deal is designed to protect the realtor, the bank, the escrow company or the builder. Ultimately YOU are the only one looking out for your best interests. **That is why you must demand everything in writing, and everything in writing must be signed, dated, time-stamped and witnessed**. There are no exceptions to this rule.

If you hear any of the phrases listed at the beginning of this chapter, warning bells should begin ringing in your head. If you are careful, and lucky, you won't need the tips I've put in Chapter 8 ("The Firm of Dewey, Cheatem & Howe").

If you are dealing with honest people they will accept these terms and the responsibility it demands of them. Honest people have nothing to hide and will be happy to earn your trust. Honest people do not try to convince you that they are honest.

NOTES:
7 DEADLY SINS: ASSESSING CHARACTER

CHAPTER 5
ESCROW IS AS ESCROW DOES

The word *escrow*, as it applies to real estate, refers to money deposited with a **third party** and released upon the satisfaction of a set of conditions. The money you hand over to an **escrow company** (the third party in the previous sentence) will be disbursed by it to the appropriate parties, upon the closing of the house you buy. Funds held in escrow are used to pay taxes and insurance premiums when they become due. Escrow is required by law and looks like a decent practice. The idea (having a **neutral third party** holding everybody accountable until successful completion of the home buying process) just seems like good business. Right?

Let me tell you a little more about what escrow *is*...and then we'll talk about what escrow *does*.

The amount of money that you will have to come up with for escrow and closing depends on several factors, including the cost of the house that you want to purchase and the type of mortgage you contract. Generally speaking, you will need to come up with enough cash to cover three costs.

1. The first cost...the very first dollars out of your pocket, are considered **earnest money.** Earnest money is the deposit you make when you submit the offer on the home you want to buy. You must prove to the seller that you are serious about wanting to buy the house. The seller or the seller's real estate agent may want to require that a portion of the earnest money be non-refundable. This is not a good

37

idea. If you are serious about buying the home in question, go ahead and offer MORE earnest money but do not agree to any of this "non-refundable" nonsense. The seller will have to accept that you are putting your money where your mouth is: your cash and your word will have to be good enough to prove that you are, indeed, earnest.

2. The second cost associated with closing escrow is the **down payment**. This is simply a percentage of your new home's purchase price. The bigger the down payment, the smaller the mortgage payment.

3. The third and final cost is a bundle called the **closing costs**. These are the costs associated with processing the paperwork to buy a house. Sometimes, sellers will offer to pay or "waive" the closing costs as part of the deal, but be aware: there is no such thing as a free lunch. Assume that the sellers are recouping the cost of their generosity somewhere else in the deal.

To summarize, escrow is a good idea. When you make an offer on a home, your earnest money will be put into an escrow account. If the offer is accepted, your earnest money will be applied to the down payment or closing costs. If your offer is not accepted, your money will be returned to you in full. This is what escrow *is*.

Now…allow me to discuss what escrow *does*.

Escrow companies are dependant upon the repeat business brought in by referrals from real estate agents. The market is too big and there is too much competition to simply rely on "walk-in" business. So, immediately, a clear and compromising relationship is established: escrow companies want to please as many realtors as possible. This is not to say that *your* realtor will have a conflict of interest between finding you the best deal available and padding the pockets of the escrow company. But the triangle of the *Seller's Realtor*, the escrow company and you is not equilateral. This kind of triangle resembles a dunce cap...and you get the short side at the bottom.

Referrals are the lifeblood of the escrow business and escrow companies do what they can to attract realtors. Escrow companies sometimes accommodate an unusual condition, arrangement or strategy that a realtor concocts to sweeten the deal for his client. Escrow companies also do all they can to project "the successful look." Some realtors judge a good deal on appearance. This, of course, can work to your advantage when you're selling your home. Just keep in mind that the appearance and the ability do not always match up. While at the escrow office, remember the mantras: "**caveat emptor**" ("let the buyer beware") and "**do not trust, do not trust, and do not trust.**" The bigger your purchase, the more your awareness and skepticism should come into play.

The person you will have the most contact with at the escrow company is the "Escrow Officer." It will seem as if this perky-petite woman with the power suit and French manicured nails is the principle administrator of your escrow affairs. Okay, MY Escrow Officer was this perky-petite woman... yours may be different. Maybe you'll get the fraternity brother with the brand new haircut, three-piece suit and spit-shine shoes. Either way the Escrow Officer is one of about a dozen employees that will be handling your business transaction, and he, most likely, will be the best-groomed and least experienced individual in the office. Chances are good, that just last week, your Escrow Officer was waiting tables at your local *Eggplant Garden* restaurant.

This individual is armed with a handful of ink pens and a seven-inch-thick stack of important looking documents printed on sheets of papers in a number of sizes. Escrow companies produce documents on odd sizes of paper not normally available to the public. Presumably, this is to emphasize their importance…as if the load of legalese mumbo-jumbo contained in those documents is not enough of an attention-getter. Ninety-nine percent of this massive stack of paper protects the escrow company, the lending bank and the realtors. One percent might actually have something to do with protecting you.

The Escrow Officer's job is box checking [ ]. Box checking [x] and on-the-line initialing __B.M.__ are his areas of expertise… along with excellent posture and grooming. It is your responsibility to question his work in detail. The Escrow Officer will ensure that all of your boxes [ ] are checked so you should make sure that all of his boxes [ ] are checked. Take into account that this four-hour box [ ] checking session could end up costing you thousands of dollars. So do not take the boxes [ ] lightly.

This bulky heap of documents is a binding contract. All the boxes and initials add up to an agreement that all parties must adhere to. Make it clear to the Escrow Officer that the escrow company may not…WILL NOT…record and deed your new home if any changes have been made to the contract. All changes must be signed and dated by you. They might even require a bit more box [ ] checking.

Ask as many questions as you'd like. Do not expect the Escrow Officer to be able to answer them, but do not accept, "I'll check on that and get back to you later." Instead, insist that Ms. French Manicure or Mr. Brand New Haircut find somebody in the office with experience and answers before you sign and initial any document you do not understand.

Bud's Five Rules

of Escrow Facilitation

1. Do not agree to give non-refundable earnest money to anybody. Money given in earnest is a promise...not a gift.

2. Assume no free lunches. (If the waiter at the *Eggplant Garden* is also your Escrow Officer... well then maybe you can get free breadsticks.)

3. Realize that your Escrow Officer will not be able to answer any questions. Insist that he fetch a professional to explain any legalese that you do not understand.

4. Instruct the Escrow Officer, in writing, that you will not provide the final signatures if ANY changes have been made to the contract without prior approval. Remember, you can request time to consider the changes. You do not have to approve the changes on the spot.

5. Do not trust, do not trust and do not trust.

NOTES:
ESCROW IS AS ESCROW DOES

CHAPTER 6
IT'S A MYSTERY

Our dream home, which soon became our monsoon mansion, was not legally "occupiable" even before the flooding. That is to say that when the escrow office authorized the closing, it had no legal basis to do so. Confused?

You will recall that on July 2, a bank employee decided (without informing us) that there was no way our real estate transaction would close before the 4th of July weekend. Acting on that assumption, the banker (whom I refer to as **2 of 10**) cancelled the homeowner's policy, or rather, had it "delayed" so it would not become effective until after the holiday weekend. Technically, **2 of 10** was right: the transaction never would have closed that day if a forgery had not occurred.

In order for the escrow office to sign off on the closing of escrow it needed a Certificate of Occupancy from the County. As of July 3, one had not been issued. Yet somehow…it's a mystery…the escrow office received an official Certificate of Occupancy that week; just hours before the entire disaster became our legal responsibility. As it turns out, the Certificate of Occupancy that the escrow office received was a forgery.

Nobody at the escrow office could recall how the office came into possession of the forged document. All they could recall is that *somebody* delivered it to the office.

So, who was this mysterious *somebody*?

1) Was it the builder's wife?

2) Was it the Builder's Realtor?

3) Was it Colonel Mustard (from a popular board game) in the library with the candlestick?

Let's take a look at the Builder's Realtor first. In his own words (under oath) that realtor said:

"I did special assignments for the builder in exchange for additional listings."

The Realtor's own words sound incriminating. What exactly did these "special assignments" entail? Did the Builder's Realtor sneak into the escrow office, hide behind the silk plants in the corner and surreptitiously plant the bogus document on the receptionist's desk when nobody was looking? Would the Realtor risk his license and livelihood in order to make a few extra bucks? Although realtors are known to go the extra mile for their clients…it is highly unlikely that he would have taken this kind of risk for the builder.

The builder, himself, was in court at the time. Could he have personally delivered the phony Certificate of Occupancy to the escrow office? The builder really needed that Certificate of Occupancy to show up when it did. He needed the deal to go through because he needed our money…and the bank's money on our behalf. The Escrow Officer had tried earlier to reach the builder, but because the unscrupulous jerk was in court (dealing with another mess he had apparently caused) the Escrow Officer was only able to reach the builder's wife.

The escrow agent explained to the builder's wife that the house could not be recorded and closed until all the papers were in order. And the Escrow Office was still missing the Certificate of Occupancy.

There was no way for the builder or his wife to come up with an actual Certificate of Occupancy, because that would have required a County official to have inspected the house. And the house would never have passed occupancy inspection because it had failed the plumbing inspection.

Nevertheless, an hour later an envelope mysteriously appeared on the receptionist's desk at the escrow office. What do you suppose was in this envelope? Yes, it was a forged Certificate of Occupancy...just exactly what the escrow office needed to close the deal. The lot number on the forged Certificate of Occupancy was incorrect, but the escrow officer missed the error.

Okay, now let's take a look at Colonel Mustard. Colonel Mustard claims he was in the study at the time, awaiting the arrival of tea and guests. Professor Plum and Ms. Peacock confirm they had an appointment with the Colonel, but they were running late as they had run out of gas en route. What was the Colonel doing during that time, and is it possible he could have made the round trip? The esteemed Colonel does appear to be operating in his own time zone...witnesses have described him as an oddity with a turn-of-the-century moustache. And, regardless of the weather, he is always wearing a pith helmet–just big enough to conceal an envelope.

NOTES:
IT'S A MYSTERY

CHAPTER 7
THINGS CAN ALWAYS GET WORSER

A long, long time ago…in a land called California…

I was in college, my hair was not yet grey, my eyes were still bright with wonder, and I had a professor who insisted that there was "no such word as worser." I didn't put up much of an argument. I took it upon faith that the professor was correct and as bad as things can get…they can only get worse. And that's the worst they can get.

Now, fast forward…to the modern era…grey hair and furrowed brow. I was standing in the business office of my insurance agent. His smallish rented space without direct sunlight featured an AM radio that lost reception if you stood too close to the doorway. As I entered, he bid me to walk swiftly away from the door so that he wouldn't miss a word of the radio broadcast. He was always very concerned with his reception. I noticed that his eyes were fixed on the checkbook in my hand. He was always very concerned with my checkbook.

I was there to pay my bill. As was the custom, our conversation began with minor chit chat regarding our personal lives.

"How's the family?"

"Taking any vacation time this year?"

"How is your mother holding up?"…etc. etc. etc.…

While writing out my check, I asked my agent about all the

junk mail I'd been getting lately that advertised discounted insurance rates. Certain insurance companies had been claiming that they could save me hundreds of dollars per year. I asked him why I should remain a client of his. He had a very polished answer ready:

"I do not sell price. I sell service. And when disaster strikes: that is the business I am in. I will be there to walk you through the insurance maze and even hold your hand. And I will be there for you. With me...you are not just a number among millions of numbers. You do not want to be represented by a claim rep that does not know how to pronounce the word "Oregon." You do not want to do business, with some voice over the phone, that is not sure what ocean borders the state you live in."

His answer made sense to me. I wanted that personal attention, and I was willing to pay for it. But I didn't just get insurance. I got a lie...and worse.

First, the worst part: the violation of trust. When I wrote that check to my agent...I paid for an opportunity to have my trust violated. I also bought a pack of lies that cost me dearly, in terms of financial loss. But to place my hope, faith and confidence in another person, and then have all of that squashed is worse. I had picked a loser for an insurance agent, but I paid my premiums for fifteen years. Which makes him the winner... and me the loser.

Even worse was the lie that his business was built on. His intentions were lies and his motivations were lies: everything that he told me to support his business was untruthful. My insurance agent was not in business to "hold my hand." He was in business to empty my pocket.

What I did not know then (but I know now)...was that my insurance agent, in insurance terms, was a *captive agent*. Which put simply means: his loyalty was to the parent company and not to the client.

At 4:48 PM Pacific Daylight Savings Time, on July 3, 2001, our dream home closed and the title was recorded (with the help of some forged papers). My wife and I had the keys handed to us at 5:00 PM July 3, 2001. By 8:00 PM, that very night, our home flooded and our insurance man informed us that we had no insurance.

Our dream home's first water bill showed that 5,840 gallons poured into our new home on July 3. And we had no insurance. And we had nobody to hold our hand. We had lots of people pointing fingers at each other. We had inspectors from three different insurance firms with lots of opinions on the damage. We had the bank and we had the escrow company explaining how they were not to blame. We had two realtors and seven lawyers. But we had nobody to hold our hand.

My "I will be there for you agent" never did show up.

We were, in fact, so shocked by the treatment that we received from our insurance agent that we included him in our litigation. We thought we could sue an insurance agent for defaulting on the coverage that he promised to provide, for the losses we incurred, for the gross mistreatment we received and for the abuse of every human right we thought we had. But human rights and legal rights are two entirely different things. Violation of trust is an emotional foul. And judges rely on juries to decide on cases involving the human element. But there are no judges or juries, or peers of any kind, in the process of deposition. There are only lawyers. Lots of lawyers.

...Oh so many lawyers.

And that entire week...I kept thinking about how much worse things really can get. They can always get worser.

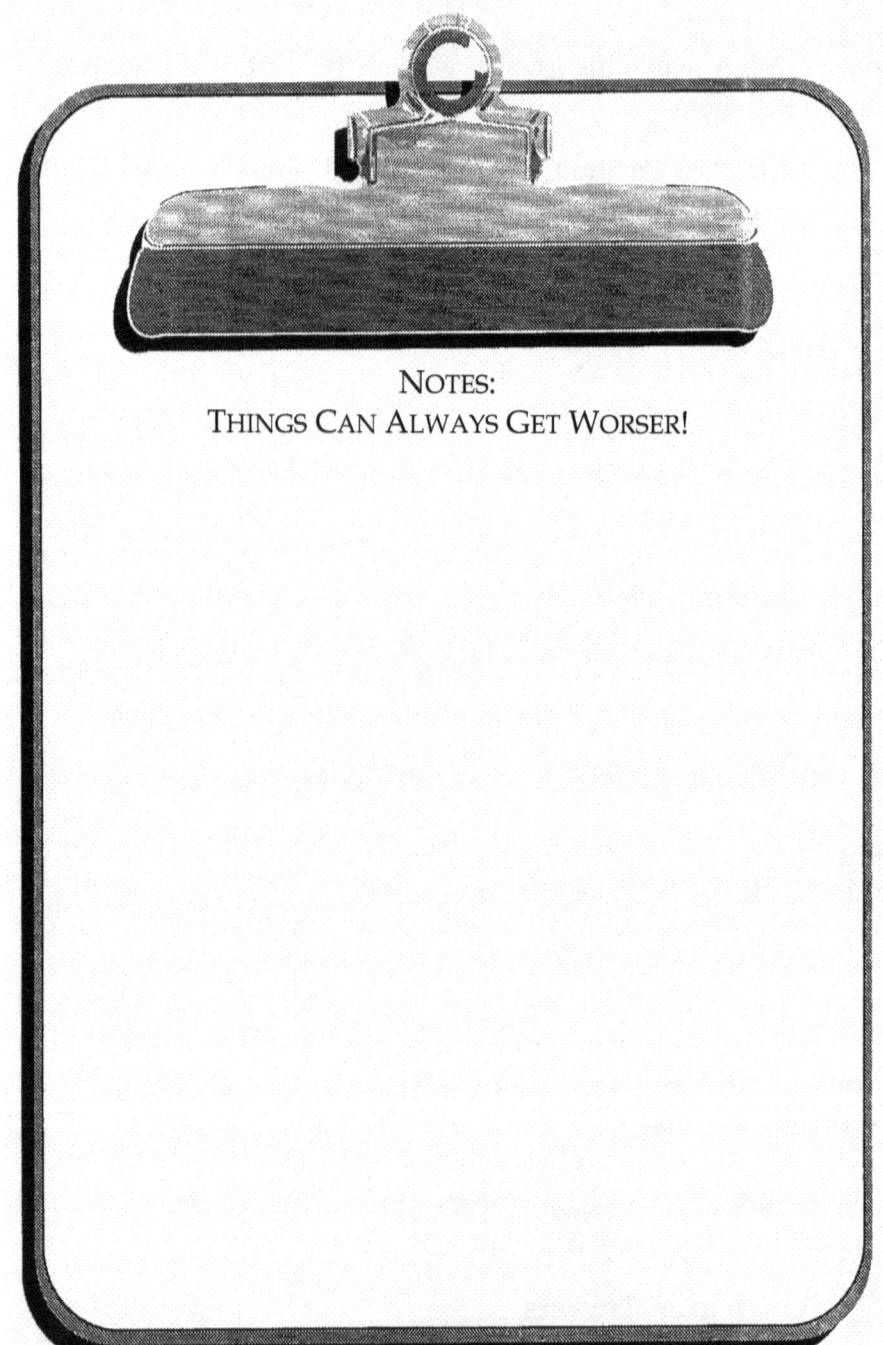

NOTES:
THINGS CAN ALWAYS GET WORSER!

CHAPTER 8
THE FIRM OF DEWEY, CHEATEM & HOWE

> **Side Bar**...hmm, we're in trouble here. Choppy waters and wicked winds, thunder clouds and nasty rains...and something sinister, with a greedy glimmer in its eye, is circling the life boat..."Honey, I think we might need a lawyer."

Or is that what's circling the raft?

At one point in our adventure we were in litigation against four insurance companies and, potentially, seven separate litigants. We were claiming to be victims of:

- fraud

- incompetence

- misrepresentation

- dereliction of duty

- stupidity

- greed

Okay, maybe stupidity and greed are a function of the territory...we should have been prepared to ride those waves. But should we have expected a tsunami of irresponsibility? Should we have expected the sharks when there was no shoreline warning sign: *BEWARE OF SHARKS!*...?

Shortly after the flood, it was clear to us that we would not be able to navigate this course alone. And so we did what every desperate cast-away does...sent out an S.O.S. And we got us a lawyer.

Choosing a lawyer can be a complicated task. Determining whether or not one is needed...well that's easy. If something goes wrong, **YES...you do need a lawyer**. Everybody has a lawyer. Lawyers have lawyers. And the lawyers of lawyers have *teams* of attorneys. This is like deciding whether to pack an oar for your boating trip. Do you want direction...or do you want to drift? And make no mistake about it...you will drift... out to sea...where sharks make a meal of people adrift.

There are scores of lawyers in the phonebook, and each one specializes in a definite field. You don't take Viagra for a headache and a personal injury lawyer will be useless in property litigation. Some lawyers will claim that they can handle anything...these lawyers are inexperienced, delusional, stupid or greedy. And remember, stupidity and greed are what we are trying to fight here. Decide what type of lawyer you need and interview those lawyers only.

> **Side Bar**...*Did he just say "interview"? I'm treading water here...just inches away from being shark food... and I'm going to take the time to interview potential rescuers?!*

Be aware...not all pirates fly the *Jolly Roger* from their masts. The only way you're going to distinguish those lawyers that will be helpful from those that will be hostile is to discuss, person-to-person, exactly what kind of trouble you're in. You will do this by phone or by meeting, but you will have to do this. And you will have to be discriminating.

There is a price tag attached to every helping hand. The price may be determined by the framed, parchment degree behind the desk, but the value is determined by the character of the person sitting at the desk. What truly matters, when selecting a lawyer, is the individual who holds the law degree.

Set up several interviews with different lawyers to discuss your issue. I recommend you seek out a lawyer that seems to have common sense...as you see it. You're not looking for a lawyer who can convince you that he has common sense in a legal way. You are not looking for a legal expert that comes off as a technical authority and specializes in matters that are way above your head. You are looking for good old-fashioned awareness and understanding that seems reasonable to you. It is that simple. You should choose a person who will listen to you...and appears to know what you are talking about. It is not good enough to have a lawyer that can merely repeat what you have just said. A parrot can do that. (And where there is a parrot...a pirate is not far behind.) You should feel comfortable, not vulnerable, when talking to this person. And you will not retain (or give a single dollar to) this person without asking for references and checking them.

Remember, although you are the one that needs help, you are still the boss. A good lawyer will understand and respect you for taking the time to make the right decision. A conceited lawyer will not. This is a business relationship, not a courtship, and both parties should be using their heads...not their hearts. Do not let yourself be "wooed" by a lawyer's promises. Do your homework and choose wisely.

> **Side Bar**...*okay, we've spotted the rescue boat, and just in time. But the sharks are still circling. How much is this rescue going to cost me?*

Legal representation does not come cheap. You may be looking at a $300.00-$400.00 per hour price tag for services rendered. Or you may be expected to hand over up to a 40% stake in the settlement award. In our case, we were suing for hundreds of thousands of dollars and did not want to pay nearly half of the settlement to our lawyer. (We selfishly thought he already owned enough BMWs.) If you have an extra $30,000.00 in the bank, and think you can easily meet the expense of a lawyer's standard fee, it is very advisable to set up a pay-as-you-go contract, preferably on a monthly or quarterly basis. That way, when the bill is due, you can ask yourself whether you are getting the best deal for your money. These fees are coming right out of your own pocket, so it is vital that you deal with your lawyer in a businesslike fashion until you are happy with his services. Whether or not you have "money to burn," you should be aware of each service that will or might be billed at an hourly rate.

For starters, every photocopy, paperclip, envelope and postage stamp will be billed to you. But wait, there is a dedicated staff of secretaries and paralegals typing and filing and photocopying and wandering around looking for paperclips and each staff person also must be paid...by you. Calendar conflicts (personal and professional) regarding other cases, not related to yours, will cause court dates to be rescheduled. You'll pay for that too. And then there is always the "professional courtesy" that your lawyer will extend to the opposition's legal team, if for no other reason than that someday in the way off future, your lawyer will want the same "professional courtesy" extended to him for unrelated (personal and professional) matters. Oh yes, there is also your lawyer's time and effort to consider...he gets paid as well.

> **Side Bar**:....*Is your head spinning yet? Do you feel like maybe this rescue isn't going to be as cut-and-dry as you thought? Maybe you didn't realize that the legal system is a whirlpool by design. 'Round and 'round it can go. Where it stops...you can't know.*

In order to stand up and step onto firm footing…you must first steady the boat. You are the captain, and you will set the rules. Within the first fifteen minutes of your first official meeting with your potential lawyer, you must establish yourself as the confident, knowledgeable individual who might hire this attorney.

This first get-together is a "let's see if we are on the same page" meeting. There should be no charge for this meeting. You should get a verbal agreement from your lawyer that there will be no charge, and you should write it down…right there and then. "Trust" is a feel-good word that does not apply to new business relationships. Trust is earned, and your lawyer will work to earn your trust if he must…but may enjoy the financial spoils of your trust if you unconditionally hand it over. This first meeting is your chance to negotiate. Again, this is a business relationship, and you CAN negotiate. Right off the bat, I highly suggest that you negotiate a cash cap of total costs.

You should negotiate the percentage of the settlement that the lawyer will receive. Will you pay him 30% or 40% or something in between? Will your lawyer accept a flat percentage pay-out with no additional fees? If so, then you probably have a strong case. If not, maybe you should find another lawyer that believes strongly that he can win your case. Or, if BIG money is involved (and you can afford out-of-pocket expenses) agree on an hourly rate instead. But you should insist that the hourly rate not exceed a predetermined percentage of the settlement. Maybe the hourly fees will be capped at 30% of the eventual settlement amount. Or you can come up with your own custom fee structure. Perhaps you might agree on a reduced hourly rate plus a reduced settlement pay-out. For instance: half the hourly fee plus a 20% stake in the settlement award.

At any rate, both parties should be satisfied with the rates. If your reasonable ideas and/or proposals are not accepted... say, "thank you," get up from the table, and leave. You can always come back, but a lawyer who cannot respect your interests, or does not believe in the validity of your case, will not want you as a client...and you do not want him. A lawyer is a business person, and if there is a fair deal on the table that will make him money and satisfy his client...he will call you back to the negotiations. I don't mind repeating myself, because this is important: YOU are the boss in this arrangement...YOU get to decide if the terms are acceptable.

The terms of any agreement do not exist until you see them in writing, dated and signed. Setting terms in writing must happen before the first case-related letter is typed, photocopied, paper clipped, enveloped or stamped by the law firm. Because when all is said, and some is done, and the settlement has been handed down...the last thing you want to hear from your lawyer is, "did we agree on 35% or 40%?" We all have memory issues from time to time, but your lawyer's might end up costing you an extra ten thousand dollars.

You've successfully selected legal representation. This means: you now have "people." As in, "my people will get with your people." Maybe you never imagined yourself as this type of "people-person," but here you are with a horde of officially authorized legal personnel at your side. Okay, maybe it's just one guy in a wool suit. Nevertheless, behind that one guy is a committed staff of legal specialists: secretaries, interns, billing coordinators, office administrators, paralegals, advisors, partners, strategic allies...and the guy who watches over the paper clips. At the very least, I'd call that a horde. Or maybe it *is* just one guy in a wool suit with a law degree and a thriving business as a Notary Public...you chose your own lawyer. Don't blame me if you didn't get the whole horde. But whether it's one "people" or a hundred "people," they are now your "people," and they are now in your corner. And what exactly are they going to do for you? Well, mostly, they are going to help you help yourself as they take you through a bizarre and drawn-out progression of legal exercises.

For instance: *mediation*. On the record, mediation is a process in which a neutral person facilitates communication between disputants to assist them in reaching a mutually acceptable agreement...yadda yadda yadda. But what mediation can be is a dog and pony show, invented by the hardhearted and pitiless, intended to undermine and exhaust the ignorant and misguided. Your lawyer may recommend, or your contract require, that you go the mediation route so that a judge may see that you've put forth the effort to cooperate with your opposition. Keep in mind...this will be like cooperating with the Spanish Inquisition. And nothing about the process of mediation will affect the result of your arbitration case. In other words, the path of mediation follows a circular trail that takes you past various hazards but leads you right back to the start.

Mediation is a non-binding process and the *mediator* has no authority to impose a resolution of the dispute in question. Even if the mediator is a nice person with compassionate ambitions to actually reconcile your disagreement, he will only be able to offer a sheepish smile and a feeble apology if the process turns into an opportunity for your legal foes to hammer you, your loved ones and your "people" into a submissive stupor. In many cases, mediation is a hoop you must jump through to demonstrate your willingness to work towards common ground. But the rival horde, sitting across the mediation table from you, is being paid hundreds of dollars per hour and may benefit from stretching the mediation into a long process. The rival horde's objectives just *might* encourage an *unwillingness* to reach common ground.

The dedicated objective of your enemy is to find a flaw in your argument. The opposition will fire an unrelenting spray of leading questions. Its people are trained and experienced in drawing out contradictory information from your answers. Your lawyer has also been trained in mediation and will, no doubt, instruct you to answer all questions with one of three effective answers:

1. Yes
2. No
3. I do not recall.

Bear in mind that, once you've retained the services of a lawyer, you are now the employer of a dedicated professional who specializes in matters of the law...not a professional memory machine. Keep *yourself* focused at all times, and it will not matter if your lawyer gets sidetracked. Always keep your appointments, demand that your lawyer keeps his and practice "Bud's Five Rules of Positive Lawyer Control."

BUD'S FIVE RULES

OF POSITIVE LAWYER CONTROL

1. Do not trust...do not trust...do not trust. *Consider* what has been shown to you. *Judge* the facts as they are presented. *Make decisions* based on the choices given. But do not act on *faith*. **And do not trust...do not trust...do not trust.**

2. If it is not written down...it did not happen.

3. Like a journalist, always be aware of details. Ask: who, what, where, when and how? Take notes and assume nothing.

4. Business is business. Business is not friendship or courtship. You will not hurt anybody's feeling by asking for more explanation, asking for proof, asking for documentation or asking for a better deal.

5. If the first four rules of engagement are balked at by the individuals you are doing business with, call the deal "off!"

> **Side Bar**...*Rough waters and violent storms behind us...nothing but smooth sailing ahead...we've got ourselves a lawyer, and we are back on-course.*

We are back on-course right?

Wait a minute...where is this lawyer taking us?

If you have been convinced by your lawyer or required by contract (as we were) to take your case to mediation, consider: this is a first step to building a court case and nothing that happens in mediation is binding nor likely reasonable. First, do not pay any advance fees, as you will be directed to do, until you have received written conformation that all other parties involved have also paid their directed fees. Second, insist, on a written agreement that states that your fees will be refunded if the opposing parties do not play-by-the-rules of the mediation process. Insist also on a procedure for the process.

Just a reminder: mediation is a nonbinding process. Even if the opposition sign a pledge to work in "good faith"... they are not legally bound to actually deliver on that pledge. It is possible that the opposition will simply refuse to comply with the mediator's recommendation. In fact, probably the other side's aim is to go through this process for the express intent of frustrating you and/or seeing how much of a sucker you really are. You are not a sucker, and you should be prepared to demonstrate this. I know this all sounds like playground stuff, but, in our experience, the opposing lawyers pulled every pestering tactic out of their bag of aggravation until we begged for recess. Do not assume that all bullies grow up. And do not depend on your lawyer to protect you. He is only there to show the bad guys, that you do have legal representation, and that you are not afraid to use it. The truth is that once you are under the microscopes of the rival horde's crack team of question-asking infuriation specialists...you may find it useful to employ "Bud's Five Rules of Peaceful Non-Cooperation."

BUD'S FIVE RULES OF PEACEFUL
NON-COOPERATION

1. Do not be the nice guy, because the defendant's lawyers are not nice people.

2. Do not chat with the defendant's representatives...before, after, during breaks...or at any time. And by chat, I mean: weather, sports, cars, lawn care...NOTHING. No one representing the defendant is your friend.

3. If one of the opposing counsel has a cough and you have cough drops in your pocket; keep them in your pocket.

4. The answers to all questions are: "yes," "no" and "I do not recall." You cannot help yourself by giving better answers... you can only help the defendant's counsel.

5. Do not volunteer any information of any kind. This will only hurt you, help your opposition, slow down the process and cost you more money.

Notes:
The Firm of Dewey, Cheatem & Howe

CHAPTER 9
DEE'S DEPOSITION

The process of *deposition,* as it applies to a real estate arbitration procedure, involves the sworn testimony of a witness, taken before a trial, held out of court, with no judge present. The witness is placed under oath to tell the truth, the whole truth and nothing but the truth...and then, and only then, can a smarmy gaggle of lawyers start asking the witness loaded questions with the explicit intent of transforming said witness into a puddle of self-doubt. If the witness has enough self confidence and resolve to withstand the personal attacks of the lawyers...then the end result may be only extreme irritation and a jaded view of our nation's legal system.

I hope that you never find yourself as the witness in a deposition. Unfortunately, my dear wife and I did. Dee was especially exasperated by the deposition proceedings. I thought her viewpoint on the event was exceptionally telling, so I asked her to write this chapter.

DEE'S OUTLOOK

I have some experience in "official" proceedings. Through my profession, I participate in Individual Education Program (IEP) meetings. Meeting minutes and written IEPs are legal documents. Participants include parents, guests invited by parents, and school personnel (such as administrators, teachers and therapists). Meetings are scheduled on dates and at times that are convenient for the parents, because the parents have the most at stake...this is simple human courtesy. Most districts try to hire support staff to do the phoning and, scheduling. The goal of these meetings is clear and stated: "to meet the needs of the student."

All of my professional training and everyday occupational procedures incorporate one underlying tenet: respect for individual dignity. This is not a matter of "rights" or "diversity"... this is the straightforward practice of people who care about other people. This is how I sleep at night when I am forced to help make unpopular decisions. This is how I wake up in the morning and motivate myself to do it all over again. I have a clear and stated goal, and I do everything with the objective of preserving the dignity of those around me. I'm not a saint. I'm just human.

Which makes me wonder: what species are the lawyers that deposed us?

Our real estate problems (nightmares) were caused by admitted negligence and fraud. Yes, ADMITTED, deception by an unscrupulous home builder. We were unable to move into our new home because of physical troubles with the house (troubles that were covered up) and legal inconsistencies that were, later, discovered to be fraudulent. Our attorney informed us that we could only be compensated for actual dollars spent while homeless. And we played by the rules. We submitted lists and receipts.

A clerical person, a secretary or filing clerk could have easily compared receipts with lists. However, we were charged professional attorney fees for this service. This, to me, seemed like an inappropriate use of the lawyers' time and our money. We were also charged full attorney fees for the multiple phone calls and letters it takes to coordinate lawyers' schedules, schedule depositions and then accommodate unplanned changes to both. The business and personal needs of the dishonest builder's legal team outweighed any consideration for our needs. We needed a home to live in, and the lawyers needed to increase their billable hours. There was a clear, but unstated, goal: disregard the Miller's needs...because they are not protected by any particular set of rights. We were not humans anymore...we were litigants.

And as litigants, we were not given the chance to salvage any amount of personal dignity. We were living in a hotel room instead of a dream house. We had paid thousands and thousands of dollars towards the legal cause of making this nightmare go away. And we were treated with disdain and spitefulness.

During the deposition, more than 40 billable hours were used up by lawyers repeating the same questions over and over again and then discussing our duplicate answers to these carbon copy questions. As this type of event is a gathering of professional cronies, there was also much socializing and catching-up to do. We were billed for that too.

Because we had moved out of our old house, put everything in storage, and were unable to move into our new house...we were in a continual state of domestic limbo. We were unable to access most of our personal belongings.

For over 25 years I had a sewing machine and a dedicated sewing room in my home. It's a hobby, and I had promised friends I would complete a project for their wedding. I was able to transport my sewing machine to the hotel; but my irons (multiple types) and ironing board were in storage. I purchased a new iron/board set. (The hotel iron and board damaged my clothing when it spat out rusty water.) I was questioned and ridiculed for this purchase. The opposing counsel asked:

Why didn't you join a church sewing circle?

Bud, always comparison shopping, found a good deal on a six-pack of Hanes brand T-shirts at Costco. The lawyers asked us many questions about these plain white T-shirts, including:

Why didn't you go to Meier & Frank, purchase just a single Fruit-of-the-Loom T-shirt and just wash it every night?

We purchased an adjustable writing table for under $70.00 because the desk in the hotel room was much too high for me. The lawyers asked:

Why didn't you request multiple phone books, from the hotel management, in order to stack on the provided chair and elevate yourself to the height of the desk provided?

It was also suggested that I use phone books to stack under my feet so that I could have reached the floor once I had climbed up on top of the tower of phone books piled on the chair.

The billable time for these ironing board, T-shirt and phone book questions added up to about $2,000.00. We paid the bill.... We had no choice. We had no home. Had we known that the sewing supplies, undergarments and writing table would have cost so much...we would have purchased higher-end products. Maybe Bud could have gotten T-shirts with pockets. It would have been less expensive if we had bought an Ethan Allen *escritoire* and not listed it for reimbursement.

We were questioned about why we felt it necessary to keep a Kosher home. It was suggested that ignoring our dietary decisions and lifestyle might have been a wiser effort on our part. However, the insurance policy that we were living off of stated that, under the circumstances, we should be able to "maintain prior lifestyle." I can see why they might have questioned a diet of caviar…but, matzoh?

The total cost to me for these deposition questions wasn't just the fees we paid to the lawyers for the privilege of being ridiculed. The higher price that we paid can only be counted in terms of our time and our dignity. The questions were based on value judgments about our lifestyle. We were not being interrogated about the validity of our reimbursement claims… we were on trial for being us.

What I understand now is that this is the tactic of the attorneys. This is how they get litigants to bend a little on their claims. This is how they make a living.

What I don't understand is…how do they sleep at night?

The attorneys were representing clients who had admitted to negligence and fraud. But we paid for the crime… financially, physically and emotionally. The ridicule we were subjected to was just too much to take. We asked to settle the case to avoid further depositions…to avoid further emotional harm…to avoid the mounting attorney fees.

In the end, we were not willing to pay the price of being right, which is exactly what the legal system appeared to us to be set up to accomplish.

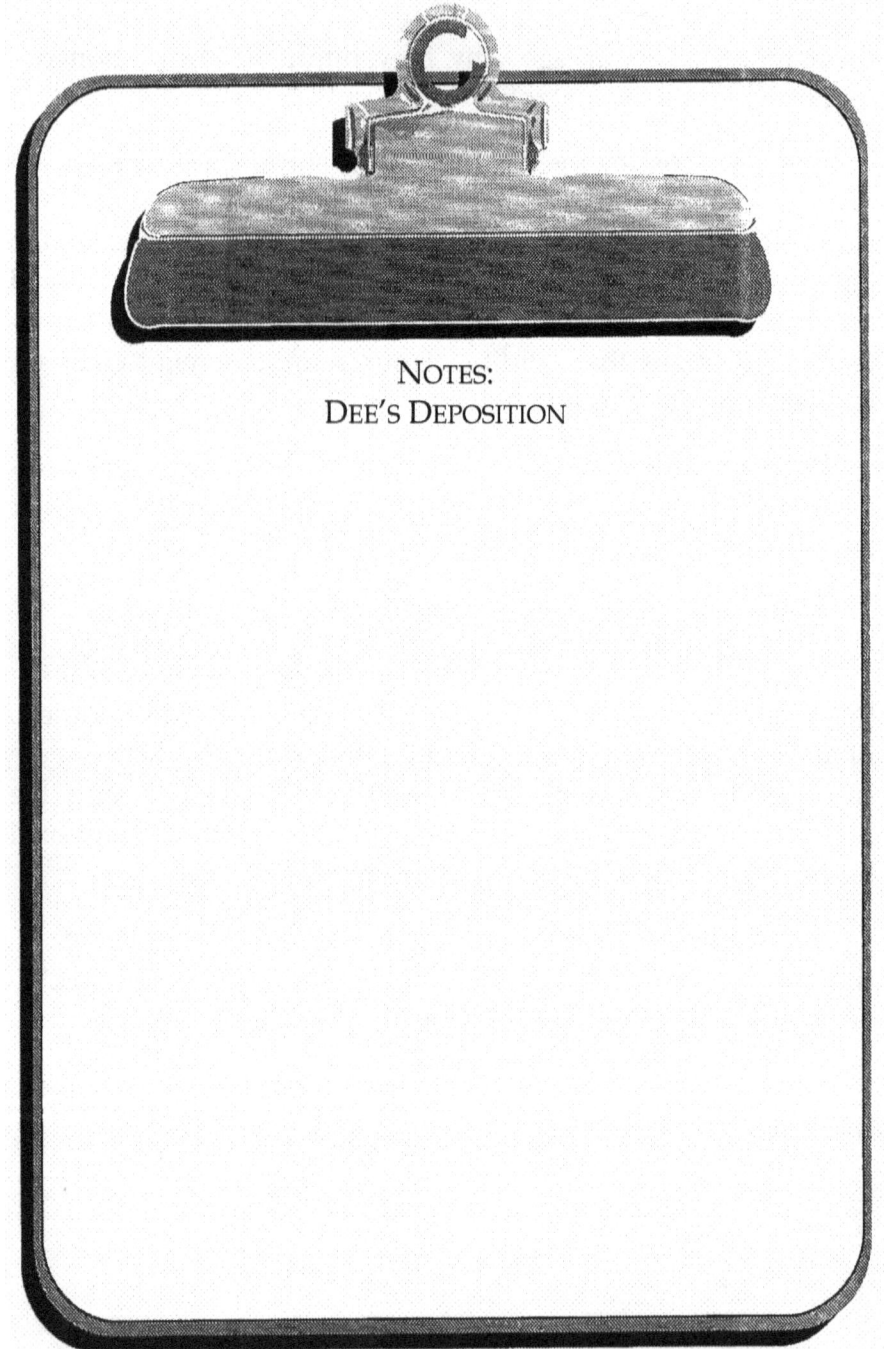

NOTES:
DEE'S DEPOSITION

CHAPTER 10
SHOW ME THE MONEY

Yes I am very emotional. About what? Well just about everything. Let me paint you a picture:

It is deposition day for me. Dee was hammered by Marsha Malicious all day yesterday with the court reporter (Carrion Flower) taking down every word. Dee had suffered the presence of overpaid graduates of the Sadism School of Law.

An elderly lawyer is deposing me. This lawyer speaks like maple syrup oozing out of a New England tree in December. It took him ten minutes to make his introduction, which consisted of saying his name and re-explaining the rules; stating that if I did not understand any question he would gladly repeat it.

Like there were three possibilities of that:

1. Slim
2. Fat
3. None

I was not having Mr. Maple Syrup repeat any question. The hours were grueling. At some point late in the afternoon, he presented a paper I had signed on the date of the escrow closing. It was my signature, and what I had read and read again having something to do with the bank's property inspection. (It was, you know, one of those many forms that are whipped passed you at signing, that just about nobody reads and that is truly a boiler plate addition to the seven-inch pile of paper on the Escrow Officer's desk.)

As you may have already guessed, Mr. Maple Syrup represented the bank. For the life of me I could not understand what this form had to do with the fact that a bank staff member instructed my insurance representative to cancel my homeowners insurance.

Five to eight minutes must have elapsed, when the bank's lawyer asked me, "Mr. Miller, do you know how to read?"

My blood boiled! I was just about to flip open my cell phone and dial 911 to make my point when my lawyer called for a time out.

At the end of the day when we all left the building, the sun had set and the streets of Portland were dark. I had a screaming, "hissy" melt down. It was not smart, but I am only human. The lawyers had insulted me, bullied my wife and tried to intimidate both of us. And the companies we were up against were paying them well to do it: $400.00 per hour times five lawyers times eight hours. Calculator not at hand? O.K. the answer is $16,000.00 per day.

"The plaintiff rests."

NOTES:
SHOW ME THE MONEY

CHAPTER 11
WE ARE SUCH LOSERS: WE LOST TWICE!

Our once-trusted, friend-to-the-family, honest-as-the-day-is-long, insurance agent proved that he could not be trusted. And even if he knew the names of my children...he was not my family's friend. And every summer has its winter.

We went through deposition for months. We answered questions and responded to accusations from a seemingly unending stream of lawyers. The last lawyer to depose us was the lawyer representing our insurance agent's malpractice insurance company. As the deposition came to a close, we realized the sad irony of our legal system:

The law benefits the lawyers, and only the insurance agents are truly insured. The malpractice insurance lawyer offered us no settlement for our loss.

At this juncture, we had to make a decision. Should we drop the case and stop the financial hemorrhaging? Or should we go to court?

We felt that we had a case. Sad ironies aside, we believed in the legal system. After spending many thousands of dollars and dozens of sleepless nights, our case ended with a summary judgment...against us. Which meant that the judge, interpreting only the letter of the law, decided that a captive insurance agent owed loyalty to the parent company, not to the client. We did not have a legal leg to stand on. In the eyes of the law the emotional impact of our loss did not matter. There would be no trial with a jury of our peers. There would be no consideration of our losses. We had now lost our dream home and our faith in the legal system.

We still did not give up.

We took our woes to appellate court. Our case was evaluated by three judges that only spoke to the lawyers involved... behind closed doors. A ruling in our favor would have only reversed the summary judgment. We waited hopefully for six months. If the summary judgment had been reversed, we would have had the opportunity to go back to square one, spend more money and see another judge.

We lost again.

We learned that neither our lawyer, nor our desire to be treated fairly, was any defense against our insurance company's insurance company and its lawyer's lawyers. We concluded that the legal system is not set up to help people.... It is an uneven contest. That's why cases are "won" or "lost."

So the bottom line is that really bad things can happen to good people. Folks that you are supposed to trust will lie to you, and the "American Dream" is used in corporate advertising as a ploy to vacuum cash out of your pockets. Nothing in the glossy brochure is an actual promise.

Maybe the three Appellate judges did us a favor. Because anger and disappointment was almost instantly replaced with "common" sense and reality.

We weren't losers.... We didn't win...but we never had a chance.

The single most important idea that I'd like to convey with this book...the dogma that I'm trying to pass on is... business relationships, of any kind, are not the same as personal relationships.

CHAPTER 12
CONCLUSION: IT WOULD BE TOO EASY

It would be too easy to declare that...because everybody seems to have his own agenda..."everybody is untrustworthy." I'm not going to say that. It may be true; maybe. That's something that you'll have to decide for yourself. But I simply do not care for a policy of not trusting anybody: too much effort. Granted, I don't enjoy feeling like a big sucker, but nor do I want to incur unnecessary chiropractic expenses from having spent too much time looking over my shoulder.

I prefer to believe in myself. I prefer to believe in humankind...of which I am a rank-and-file member. And I am trustworthy; therefore some others must also be trustworthy. Well, that's the logic I'm working with, anyway.

I once sold a house that was infested with carpenter ants. I didn't know they were there...they had not introduced themselves to me. The realtor and the private home inspector that were part of the home's sale did not know they were there. These uninvited guests were discovered by the new owners. They had stowed away underneath the carpet. They had not been visible to the "naked eye." And because their presence was a big secret...the "full disclosure" act just did not apply. I am a trustworthy person. But try telling that to the folks who purchased the carpenter ants from me.

As it turns out, untrustworthy people (a.k.a. business sharks) operate with an unhealthy "what's in it for me" ethic. Unbeknownst to me, the house I sold had ants. The house I bought was infested by deceit. The very nature of chance, circumstance and assorted "acts of God" assure us that we will never be in enough control to know everything fully. However, some people have no compunction about deceiving others in order to turn a profit. The intention of making more money than your fellow man does not balance well upon the bases of truth and full disclosure. I had to learn that the hard way.

Call me simple, ignorant or naïve, but I set out as a pilgrim on the road to the American Dream, blithely unaware that I would meet up with opportunistic thugs (with business cards) making a living by waylaying travelers along the way.

There are laws against this type of "highway robbery," but when it comes to real estate transactions "full disclosure" laws have very few teeth. The sobering truth is that bigger teeth are found in the laws protecting those professionally-affiliated with real estate transactions. Laws do exist to protect simpletons like me from "partial disclosure," but the protection is better for businesses than for individuals.

Thus, it is even more important to be knowledgeable before entering into a real estate transaction.

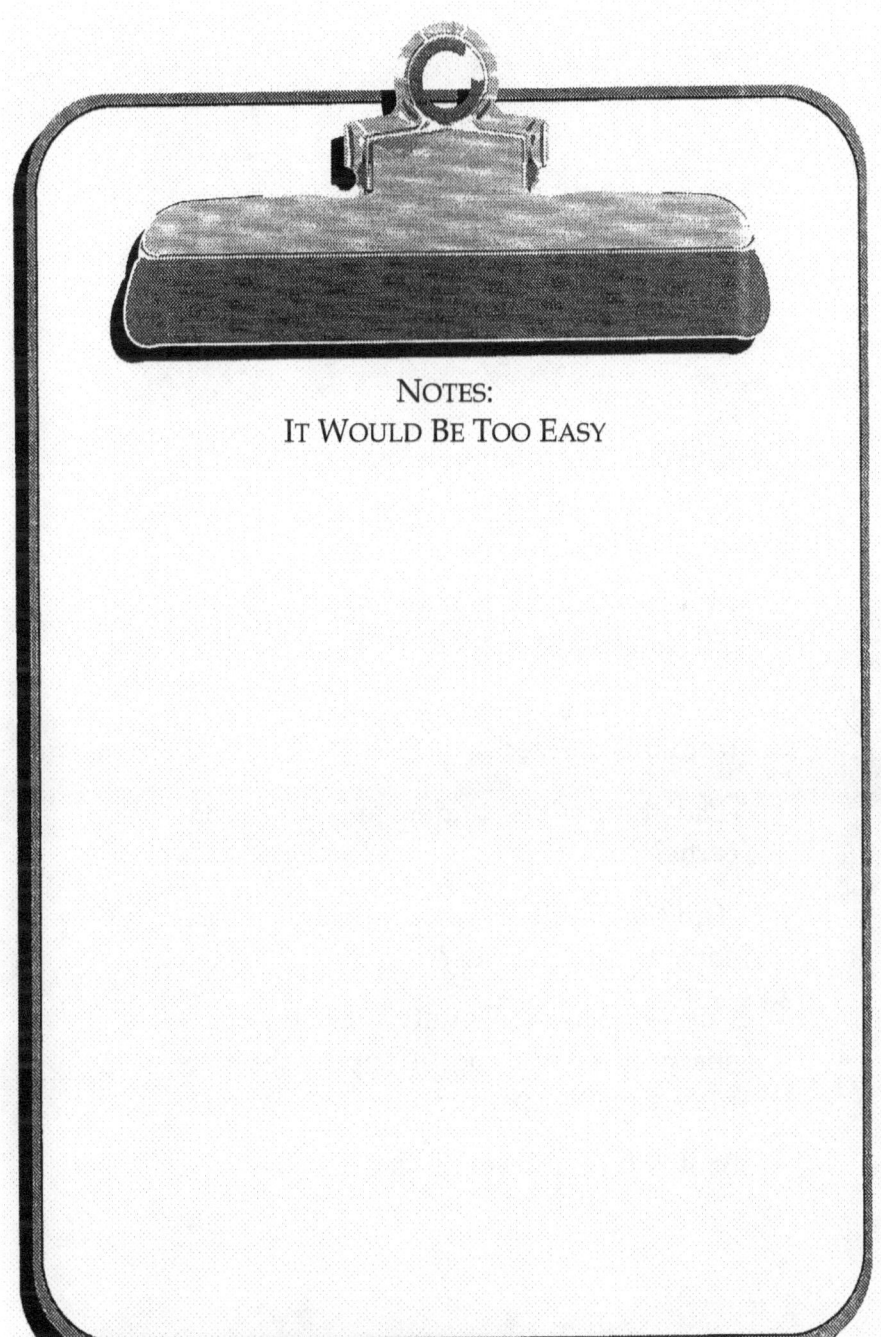

NOTES:
IT WOULD BE TOO EASY

APPENDIX A

DO I HAVE...?

☐ Current information from the County about the builder's license and liability insurance?

☐ Multiple references with answers to specific questions such as:

-Would you purchase another home from this builder?

-Did the builder understand your concerns?

-Did the builder correct problems in reasonable time periods?

☐ Copies from the County (or City) of inspection reports and, if applicable, Certificate of Occupancy?

☐ Bank information compiled?

☐ Realtor information compiled?

☐ Contractor/Builder information compiled?

☐ Insurance Policy information compiled?

☐ Escrow Policy information compiled?

☐ Document files organized and available?

DID I REMEMBER?

☐ If it is not written, it did not happen.

☐ To ask: Who? What? When? Where? Why? How?

☐ It is business not friendship.

☐ To stay in control.

☐ Before I sign anything, did I read it? Did I understand it?

FOR THE RECORD

INITIAL INFORMATION

NAME OF BUSINESS:

PHONE:	**TOLL FREE #:**
DATE:	**TIME:**
GOAL:	

CONTACT:

SUPERVISOR:

LOCATOR #:

RESERVATION #:

REPAIR AUTHORIZATION:

CREDIT CARD APPROVAL #:

RESULT:

FOLLOW UP NEEDED:

NOTES:
DO I HAVE...?

APPENDIX B

CODE AND GUIDE

2005 REALTORS CODE OF ETHICS AND STANDARDS OF PRACTICE

Visit the National Association of Realtors website at: http://www.realtor.org and type "Code of Ethics" into the search box. Or go directly to:

http://www.realtor.org/mempolweb.nsf/pages/code

MOVING GUIDE

Most realty companies produce a useful, general guide for clients who are preparing to move. If you have not already received one, ask your realtor for his standard moving guide.

NOTES:
CODE & GUIDE

APPENDIX C

RECORDS

☐ Building Permits

☐ Inspection Reports

☐ Contracts

☐ Escrow Papers

☐ Banking Receipts

☐ Contact Information for Subcontractors

☐ Appliance Instructions and Warranties

☐ Insurance Policies

☐ Banking Papers

☐ Utility Contact Information

Escrow Papers
Insurance Policy
Phone Numbers

Not packed in boxes

Not in moving truck

Keep your documents organized!
Keep them accessible!
If it is not written it does not exist!

INDEX

90

www.ingramcontent.com/pod-product-compliance
Lightning Source LLC
Chambersburg PA
CBHW031245280526
45784CB00004B/1732